10P

Life and Times

Queen Victoria

John Malam

WAYLAND

Titles in the Life and Times series:

Florence Nightingale • Queen Elizabeth I
Queen Victoria • William Shakespeare •

Editor: Liz Gogerly
Consultant: Norah Granger
Cover designer: Jan Sterling
Designer: Joyce Chester
Production controller: Carol Stevens

First published in 1999 by Wayland Publishers Limited
61 Western Road, Hove, East Sussex BN3 1JD

British Cataloguing in Publication Data
Malam, John
1. Victoria. – (Life and times)1. Victoria, Queen of
Great Britain –Juvenile literature
2. Queens – Great Britain – Biography – Juvenile
literature
3. Great Britain – History – Victoria, 1837–1901 –
Juvenile literature
I. Title
941'. 081' 092

ISBN 0 7502 2292 1

Typeset in England by Joyce Chester

Printed and bound in Italy by
G. Canale & C.S.p.A Turin

Picture acknowledgements

The publishers gratefully acknowledge the following
organizations for allowing their pictures to be
reproduced in this book: Bridgeman Art Library/Forbes
Magazine Collection 4/ Guildhall Library 5, 7, 12/
Bradford Art Galleries and Museums 8/ Crown
Estate/Institute of Directors 10/ Victoria and Albert
Museum 17/ John Bethell 21/ Science Museum 27;
Hulton Getty 5, 11, 15, 20, 25; Mary Evans 6, 7, 9, 16,
20, 22, 23, 24, 28, 29 (top & bottom); Peter Newark 13
(top & bottom); Robert Harding 14; Robert Opie 9, 15,
23, 27; Neill Bruce 26; Wayland/Norfolk Museum's
Service 18 (bottom), 18 (top), 19, 25.

Find Wayland on the Internet at http://www.wayland.co.uk

All Wayland books encourage children to
read and help them improve their literacy.

✓ The contents page, page numbers,
headings and index help locate
specific pieces of information.

✓ The glossary reinforces alphabetic
knowledge and extends vocabulary.

✓ The further information section
suggests other books dealing with the
same subject.

✓ Find out more about how this book
is specifically relevant to the National
Literacy Strategy on page 31.

Contents

An exciting new era

 A young Queen Victoria, dressed for the opera.

Firsts in Britain in the 1830s
1837 First railway tickets sold
1838 First parachute jump by an Englishman
1839 First bicycle made

In 1837 Britain had a new queen. Her name was Victoria. She was queen for the next 64 years. During her long life, Victoria saw many changes in the world around her.

▲ The first railways in Britain were built in the 1830s.
Before railways people travelled by horse and carriage.

It was a time of inventions and discoveries. Some of these changed the way people lived for ever. Life was exciting, but it could be hard too.

Very poor people lived in rotten, damp houses without clean water. Some people could not afford shoes. ▶

Princess Victoria is born

One summer morning in 1819, a baby girl was born in Kensington Palace in London. Her name was Alexandrina Victoria or Princess Victoria. When she grew up she would become the Queen of England.

◄ Princess Victoria, aged 2, with her mother.

▲ Kensington Palace where Princess Victoria lived as a child. It was surrounded by gardens.

Life for Princess Victoria was simple and happy. She enjoyed playing with her dolls. She also loved to dance and sing, read books and draw pictures.

Princess Victoria aged 11 with her drawing book and dog. ▶

Long live the Queen!

When Princess Victoria was just 18 years old her life suddenly changed. Her uncle, King William, died and she was now Queen Victoria. The young queen was immediately popular with her people.

The crown was placed on Victoria's head at her coronation. ▼

Victoria was crowned at Westminster Abbey. Inside, people called out 'God save Queen Victoria!' as the crown was placed on her head.

Outside, the sound of trumpets and drums filled the air, crowds cheered and cannons were fired.

▲ Souvenirs were made of Queen Victoria's coronation, such as this mug.

◄ Britain was the first country to use postage stamps. Queen Victoria was the first person shown on a stamp.

Victoria and Albert

When Victoria met her handsome cousin, Albert, she soon fell in love with him. The young prince from Germany was shy and Victoria asked him to marry her. They were married the next year.

Prince Albert. Victoria said he was 'quite charming' and 'handsome'. ▶

Albert did not speak English very well, and many people did not like him. But Albert was good at organizing things and he helped Victoria with her duties. They loved each other very much and were always happy together.

Victoria and Albert's Christmas tree in 1848. Six of their children are with them. ▶

Britain in the 1850s

Prince Albert had a wonderful idea.
He helped to organize an exhibition
of all the latest British inventions.
It was called the Great Exhibition.
It showed that Britain
was the 'workshop of
the world'. Victoria was
very proud of Albert.

Firsts in Britain in the 1850s
1850 First hippopotamus came here
1852 First pillar box set up
1853 First chocolate bar made
1855 First public toilets opened
1856 First photograph taken underwater
1859 First children's playground opened

▲ The Great Exhibition was held inside the Crystal Palace. It was
a huge hall made from glass and iron, just like a greenhouse.

Sadly, the 1850s was also a time of trouble. Soldiers from Britain were sent to fight wars in Russia and India.

▲ The Victoria Cross was first given to brave soldiers who fought in the Crimean war in Russia.

◀ British soldiers fighting in the Crimean war.

Getting away from London

In London, the Royal Family lived in Buckingham Palace. Victoria said it was a cold house. Sometimes, Victoria and Albert wanted to get away from the busy city to spend more time with their family.

Buckingham Palace as it is today. Victoria never really felt at home there. ▼

They decided to buy two holiday homes. They were Osborne House on the Isle of Wight and Balmoral Castle in Scotland. The Royal Family spent many happy times in both places.

▲ The Royal Family in the royal train on their way to Balmoral Castle.

▼ The Royal Family at Balmoral after a stag hunt.

Families in the Victorian age

Victorian families were often large. Many people had five or more children. Victoria and Albert had nine children. Victorian parents were usually strict with their children.

▼ The Royal Family in 1861.

Children from poor families were often badly treated. Many were sent out to work for long hours. Others stayed at home to look after the younger children in the family.

▲ At the start of Victoria's reign poorer children often worked in factories. This child is a shoeshine boy.

All children go to school

Children from rich families were luckier than poor children. Nannies looked after them, and they had toys and books.

Victorian children played card and counter games, such as this game of Lotto. ▶

A governess would teach the children at home. Then, when the boys were old enough, they were sent away to school.

◀ This painting shows a family helping a boy get ready to go away to school.

Slowly, things changed for poorer children too. By the end of the Victorian age all children had to go to school. Now everybody could learn how to read and write, and how to count properly.

There are more than 50 children in this Victorian class. ▼

The year of great sadness

The year 1861 was the saddest year of Victoria's life. In March, her mother died. Then in December, Prince Albert became ill and died of a fever.

▲ Victoria and Albert enjoyed happy times together. This was the first photograph ever taken of Victoria.

◄ Victoria never forgot Albert. For the rest of her life she worked with his picture by her side.

Victoria was heartbroken. For the rest of her long life she wore black clothes to show that she missed him. For many years she hid herself away in her country homes and her people hardly ever saw her.

The Royal Albert Hall, in London, was built in memory of Prince Albert. He had dreamed about building museums and concert halls. His statue stands outside. ▼

Victoria and the British Empire

When Victoria was queen, Britain ruled many countries around the world. They belonged to the British Empire.

◀ Victoria was made Empress of India. It was a way of saying that she was the ruler of India.

At one time nearly a quarter of all the people in the world lived in the countries of the British Empire. Victoria was their queen too.

◀ British tiger hunters in India celebrate Christmas.

British people were proud of their Empire. The countries in red on this world map were part of the British Empire. ▼

ANOTHER LITTLE PATCH OF RED

BRITISH POSSESSIONS COLOURED RED.

From jubilee to jubilee

In 1887 there was a holiday because Victoria had been queen for 50 years. It was her Golden Jubilee. The queen and a procession of nobles rode through London. Crowds of people cheered Victoria all the way.

▲ The Golden Jubilee procession went from Buckingham Palace to Westminster Abbey.

Ten years later Victoria celebrated her Diamond Jubilee. She had been queen for 60 glorious years. There was another great procession in London.

▲ Thousands of people cheered Victoria during the Diamond Jubilee.

A souvenir cup and saucer for the Diamond Jubilee. ▶

Britain in the 1890s

After 1890 there were even more changes to the way people lived their lives. Motor cars and telephones were invented. Electricity worked machines in factories, and gave light to towns and homes.

The world's first motor cars were made in Germany. ▼

The telephone used by Queen Victoria at Osborne House. ▶

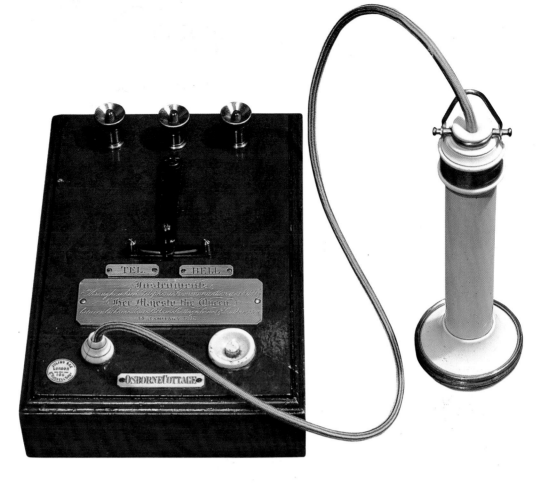

But there were also problems in the British Empire. Many soldiers died in a terrible war in South Africa.

Firsts in Britain in the 1890s
1890 First goalnets used in football matches
1891 First electric torch made
1892 First music records sold
1896 First radio signal sent
1898 First escalator fitted in a shop

◀ Queen Victoria sent special tins of chocolate to British soldiers fighting in South Africa.

The Queen is dead!

Queen Victoria died at Osborne House when she was 81 years old. She had been Queen longer than any British ruler before her. Victoria was known as the 'Grandmother of Europe'.

Queen Victoria's funeral procession. ▼

The new ruler was her eldest son, the Prince of Wales. He became King Edward VII.

◄ Edward VII was an old man by the time he became king.

▲ Victoria, surrounded by some members of her large family. She had 40 grandchildren and 37 great-grandchildren.

Important dates in Victoria's life

1819 Princess Alexandrina Victoria was born

1820 King George III died (Victoria's grandfather). George IV became the next king (Victoria's uncle). Victoria's father died

1830 King George IV died. William IV became king (Victoria's uncle)

1837 King William IV died. Victoria became queen

1838 Victoria's coronation

1840 Victoria married Albert. Their first child was born

1842 Victoria and Albert visited Scotland for the first time

1843 Victoria and Albert bought Osborne House

1847 Victoria and Albert bought Balmoral Castle

1857 Victoria's ninth, and last, child was born

1861 Victoria's mother died. Prince Albert died

1876 Victoria became Empress of India

1887 Victoria's Golden Jubilee (50 years as Queen)

1897 Victoria's Diamond Jubilee (60 years as Queen)

1901 Victoria died. Victoria's eldest son became King Edward VII

Glossary

Coronation The special time when a person is made king or queen.

Crown Placing a crown on a person's head at a coronation.

Empire Different lands all ruled together by one country.

Exhibition A display of interesting objects or paintings.

Governess A female teacher who lives in her pupil's house.

Jubilee A celebration.

Nobles People from important families.

Ruler The leader of a country.

Souvenir Specially made objects to remember special occasions by.

Further information

Books to read

Queen Victoria by Andrew Langley (Hamlyn, 1995)
Queen Victoria by Richard Wood (Wayland, 1995)
Victoria by D. Turner (Wayland, 1988)

Places to visit

Albert Memorial, London
The national memorial to Prince Albert. Unveiled by Queen Victoria in 1876.

Balmoral Castle, Scotland
Victoria's Scottish home, used by today's Royal Family. Some rooms are open to the public.

Buckingham Palace, London
Victoria's London home. It is the official home of the Queen. Some rooms are open to the public.

Holyrood Palace, Edinburgh
Contains some objects linked with Queen Victoria.

Kensington Palace, London
Victoria's birthplace. The cot used by her children is on show.

Museum of London, London
Contains Victoria's childhood toys, and her royal carriage.

National Railway Museum, York
Contains royal trains and some carriages.

Osborne House, Isle of Wight
Some rooms have been left just as they were when Victoria died there in 1901.

Victoria Monument, London
The national memorial to Victoria.

Use this book for teaching literacy

This book can help you in the literacy hour in the following ways:

- ✓ Children can re-tell the story of Queen Victoria to give the main points in sequence and pick out significant incidents.

- ✓ Teaches children the stories behind part of our heritage, including the words we use.

- ✓ Children can use the story of Victoria and her times to write fictionalized accounts of, for example, travelling on a train for the first time, or seeing the Queen pass by at one of her jubilee processions.

Index

Numbers in **bold** refer to pictures and text.